Helping Others
The Story of Fanny Jackson Coppin

In 1837, Fanny Jackson Coppin was born into slavery. Fanny was very sick as a child. She had chills and fevers. Still, she had to work. She was a slave. It was not a fair way to live.

One day, Fanny got her freedom. Her aunt gave $125 to the slave owner to set Fanny free.

When Fanny was free she was happier. But she was still not treated equally. Back then African Americans had few rights. Most had no education, so they could not get good jobs. They had to work very hard for very little money. Most African Americans were poor.

Fanny wanted to go to school so badly. She was so smart and curious. What could she do?

In Massachusetts, Fanny's aunt found a school for her. It was a school for African Americans.

"But I could not go on wash day, or ironing day, or cleaning day," Fanny said.

Still, Fanny learned how to read and write. This was a great success. Most African Americans of the time could not read or write. That was because slaves were not allowed to go to school.

Fanny went to a school to learn to become a teacher. When she graduated she wanted more. She had secretly been taking piano lessons, too. She was good at everything she did. Why wasn't she allowed to do something with her talent?

Fanny learned about Oberlin College in Ohio. It was the only college in the United States that African Americans could attend. Only one other African American woman had ever gone there. Fanny decided she would go, too. She was not afraid to be the first to do something. She was used to making her own way.

In 1860, Fanny became a student at Oberlin. It was amazing. Fanny had been born a slave,

and now she was a college student. Her
teachers could not believe it.

Fanny worked hard. She learned how to read
Latin and Greek. She took classes that only men
were allowed to take. She did things no one else
had done before. The next year, the teachers at
Oberlin asked Fanny to teach a class!

They warned her it would not be easy. No African American woman had ever taught a college class before. The students might get angry. But Fanny would not hide under her desk. She held her head high and became a teacher.

The students loved Fanny's class. They thought it was the best. Fanny was such a good teacher she taught three classes! The teachers at Oberlin were amazed.

But Fanny did not only teach college students. She started teaching a group of African American men, too. They had escaped slavery, but they had never gone to school. Fanny taught them how to read and write.

Fanny knew what she would do with her life. She would help African Americans succeed. What they needed, she believed, was an education.

In 1865, Fanny graduated from Oberlin College. The American Civil War had just ended. All the slaves were free. But Fanny saw a new problem. Without an education, African Americans could not get good jobs.

Fanny became a teacher at a school for African Americans in Philadelphia. She taught Latin, Greek, and math. In 1869, she became the principal of the school! Fanny Coppin was the first African American woman to ever have such an important job.

Fanny's students were learning well. But she worried they would not find good jobs. Fanny took the school in a new direction.

Knowing Latin and Greek would not help a man or woman get a job in a factory or in an office. Fanny wanted her students to learn certain skills.

She made the school bigger. All the students would still learn Latin, Greek, math, and English. But in Fanny's new school, they would learn much more.

"For the boys: bricklaying, plastering, carpentry, shoemaking, printing, and tailoring," Fanny said. And "stenography [taking notes] and typewriting."

"For the girls: dressmaking, millinery [hatmaking], typewriting, stenography, and classes in cooking."

Fanny's school was the first in the country to teach these skills to African Americans. The school was a success. Students graduated and found good jobs. Fanny was proud.

The years went by, and Fanny Coppin was busy as ever. For most of her life, Fanny Coppin held a round piece of chalk in her hand and taught classes. She wrote on chalkboards and taught others how to read.

Cooking class

Library at Fanny's school

Many of the students at Fanny's school were poor. They could not pay for classes. So Fanny asked people around the country to help. People saw how important the school was. They sent money to help make it run. Fanny called these people heroes.

In 1902, Fanny made sure the school was in good hands. Then she left the country. She sailed across the Atlantic Ocean to South Africa. For the next ten years, Fanny helped the poor people there find better homes and jobs.

Fanny Coppin spent her life helping others. The school where she was principal was in Philadelphia, Pennsylvania. Today, the state of Pennsylvania celebrates the life of Fanny Coppin. March 10 through March 16 is Fanny Jackson Coppin Week.

By helping others, you, too can celebrate
the life of Fanny Coppin. Look around where
you live. Does anyone need your help?